Little People™ Big Book

About
BEDTIME

Table of Contents

Time for Bed

All Tucked In

Bedtime

All day in Mother's garden here
I play and play and play.
But when night brings a dozen stars
I can no longer stay.

Sometimes the sun has hardly set
Before the stars begin.
A dozen stars come out so fast
And then I must go in.

I count them very carefully,
Especially 'round the moon,
Because I do not wish to go
To bed a star too soon.

Helen Coale Crew

In the Dark

Dream Time

Time for Bed

Going to Bed

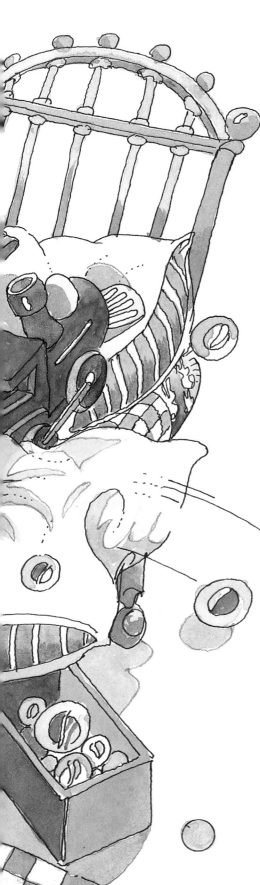

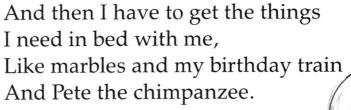

I'm always told to hurry up,
Which I'd be glad to do,
If there were not so many things
That need attending to.

But first I have to find my towel
Which fell behind the rack,
And when a pillow's thrown at me
I have to throw it back.

And then I have to get the things
I need in bed with me,
Like marbles and my birthday train
And Pete the chimpanzee.

I have to see my polliwog
Is safely in its pan,
And stand a minute on my head
To be quite sure I can.

I have to bounce upon my bed
To see if it will sink,
And then when I am covered up
I find I need a drink.

Marchette Chute

TIMMY'S BEDTIME QUESTIONS

Timmy has a lot to ask his daddy before he goes to sleep.
Maybe you have wondered about these questions, too!

Why do I have to go to sleep?
Everyone needs sleep. When you are sleeping, your body is getting the rest it needs to keep you healthy and strong.

What makes me yawn?
When you are tired, your brain needs oxygen. Oxygen is in the air. A yawn is like a big breath that sends extra oxygen to your brain. Your brain sends a signal to your lungs and your mouth that says, "Send up more air!" So your mouth opens. You yawn and take in more oxygen.

Why can't I see the sun at night?
The earth is always turning. It turns so slowly that you can't feel it. When the part of the earth where you live is facing the sun, it is daytime. All day long the earth turns away from the sun until you can't see it anymore. Then it is night. During the night, the earth turns back toward the sun. Then it is daytime again.

Is there really a man in the moon?
There is no man in the moon, but sometimes it looks as if there is. The surface of the moon is bumpy. It has mountains and valleys. The high parts of the moon cast shadows on the low parts, and sometimes the shadows look like two eyes, a nose, and a mouth—just like the face of the man in the moon!

Goldilocks and the Three Bears

A Retelling of a Traditional Story

nce upon a time there were three bears who lived in a cozy little house in the woods. There was a great big Papa Bear, a middle-sized Mama Bear, and a teeny tiny Baby Bear.

Each bear had his own bowl to eat from. Papa Bear had a great big bowl, Mama Bear had a middle-sized bowl, and Baby Bear had a teeny tiny bowl all to himself.

Each bear also had his own chair to sit in. Papa Bear had a great big chair, Mama Bear had a middle-sized chair, and Baby Bear had a teeny tiny chair all to himself.

And each bear had his own bed to sleep in. Papa Bear had a great big bed, Mama Bear had a middle-sized bed, and Baby Bear had a teeny tiny bed all to himself.

One morning the three bears woke up and filled their bowls with porridge for breakfast. But the porridge was too hot to eat, so the three bears went outside for a walk. It was a lovely day.

While they were gone, along came a little girl named Goldilocks. She looked in the window of the three bears' house. No one was home, so she opened the door and went inside.

Right away, Goldilocks noticed the three bowls of porridge. She was hungry, so she decided to taste some.

First she tasted Papa Bear's porridge, but it was too hot.

Next she tasted Mama Bear's porridge, but it was too cold.

Then she tasted Baby Bear's porridge. It was just right! So Goldilocks ate it all up.

Goldilocks wandered into the next room and saw the three bears' chairs. She decided to sit down and rest. First she sat in Papa Bear's chair, but it was too high. Then she sat in Mama Bear's chair, but it was too low. Then she sat in Baby Bear's chair. It was just right! But suddenly, it broke into pieces!

Goldilocks was very tired by this time, so she went upstairs to take a nap. There she saw the three bears' beds. First she tried Papa Bear's bed, but it was too hard. Next she tried Mama Bear's bed, but it was too soft. Finally, she tried Baby Bear's bed. It was just right! Soon Goldilocks was fast asleep.

It was not long before the three bears came home from their walk. They were hungry for their porridge. But Papa Bear looked in his great big bowl and said in his great big voice, "SOMEONE'S BEEN EATING MY PORRIDGE!"

Mama Bear looked in her middle-sized bowl and said in her middle-sized voice, "Someone's been eating *my* porridge!"

Then Baby Bear looked in his teeny tiny bowl and said in his teeny tiny voice, "Someone's been eating *my* porridge! And she's eaten it all up!"

The three bears hurried to the next room to see what else had happened while they were gone. Papa Bear looked at his great big chair and said in his great big voice, "SOMEONE'S BEEN SITTING IN MY CHAIR!"

Mama Bear looked at her middle-sized chair and said in her middle-sized voice, "Someone's been sitting in *my* chair!"

Then Baby Bear looked at his teeny tiny chair and said in his teeny tiny voice, "Someone's been sitting in *my* chair! And she's broken it to pieces!"

The three bears ran upstairs to see what else they would find. Papa Bear looked at his great big bed and said in his great big voice, "SOMEONE'S BEEN SLEEPING IN MY BED!"

Mama Bear looked at her middle-sized bed and said in her middle-sized voice, "Someone's been sleeping in *my* bed!"

Then Baby Bear looked at his teeny tiny bed and said in his
teeny tiny voice, "Someone's been sleeping in *my* bed! And here
she is!"

Baby Bear's teeny tiny voice was so sharp and shrill that it woke
Goldilocks up. And when she saw the three bears looking at her,
she jumped out of bed, raced down the stairs, and zoomed out of
the house. She ran straight home, and the three bears never saw
her again.

THIS IS THE WAY WE GO TO BED

Lori and Danny are getting ready for bed. While you read this poem, you can act out everything Lori and Danny do. Is this the way you go to bed?

This is the way we go to bed,
Go to bed, go to bed,
This is the way we go to bed
At bedtime every evening.

This is the way we brush our teeth,
Brush our teeth, brush our teeth,
This is the way we brush our teeth
At bedtime every evening.

Brush up and down.

Rub your face.

This is the way we wash our face,
Wash our face, wash our face,
This is the way we wash our face
At bedtime every evening.

This is the way Mom tucks us in,
Tucks us in, tucks us in,
This is the way Mom tucks us in
At bedtime every evening.

Pretend you're pulling up those covers.

This is the way Mom reads to us,
Reads to us, reads to us,
This is the way Mom reads to us
At bedtime every evening.

Pretend you're holding your favorite book.

This is the way we kiss good night,
Kiss good night, kiss good night,
This is the way we kiss good night
At bedtime every evening.

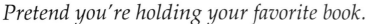

Kiss good night.

This is the way we go to sleep,
Go to sleep, go to sleep,
This is the way we go to sleep
At bedtime every evening.

Now pretend to sleep. Sweet dreams!

15

Good Night
Little People

The evening is coming, the sun sinks to rest;
The birds are all flying straight home to their nests.
"Caw, caw," says the crow as he flies overhead,
It's time little people were going to bed.

The flowers are closing, the daisy's asleep;
The primrose is buried in slumber so deep.
Shut up for the night is the pimpernel red.
It's time little people were going to bed.

The butterfly, drowsy, has folded her wing;
The bees are returning, no more the birds sing;
Their labor is over, their nestlings are fed.
It's time little people were going to bed.

Here comes the pony, his work is all done;
Down through the meadow he takes a good run;
Up go his heels and down goes his head.
It's time little people were going to bed.

Good night, little people, good night and good night.
Sweet dreams to your eyelids till dawning of light.
The evening has come, there's no more to be said.
It's time little people were going to bed.

Traditional

All Tucked In

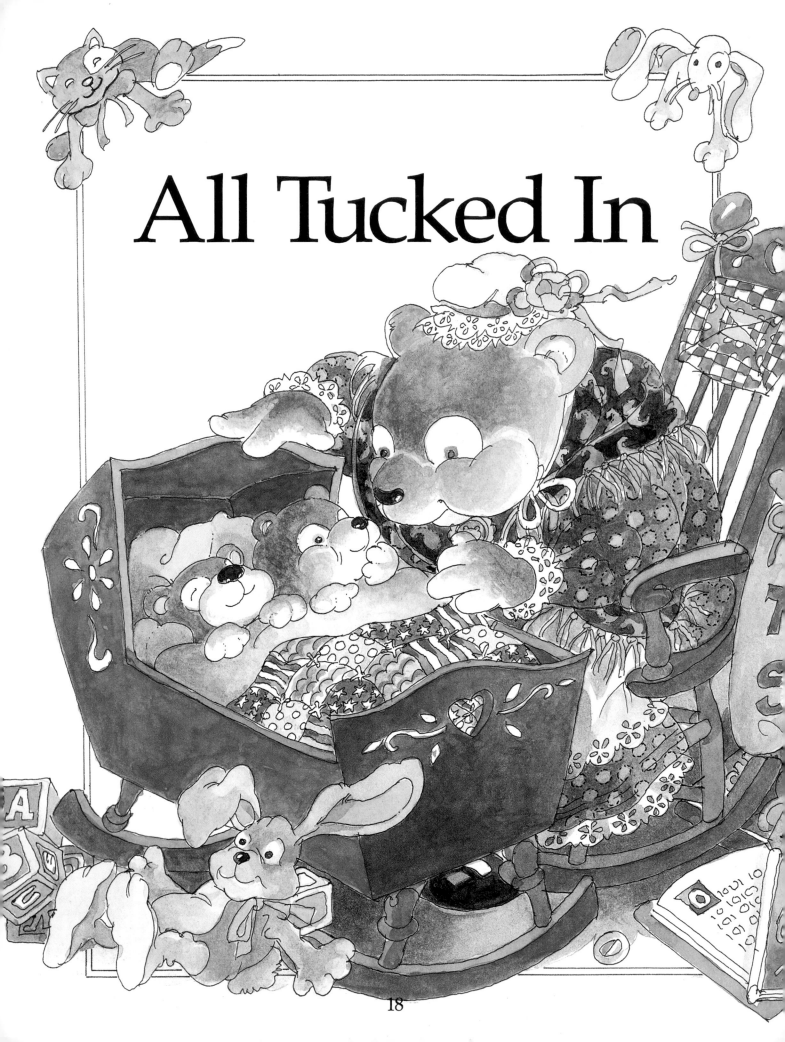

Golden Slumbers

Golden slumbers kiss your eyes,
Smiles awake you when you rise;
Sleep, pretty darlings, do not cry,
And I will sing a lullaby.

Care you know not, therefore sleep,
While over you, our watch we keep;
Sleep, pretty darlings, do not cry,
And I will sing a lullaby.

Traditional

The Princess and the Pea

A Retelling of the Fairy Tale by
Hans Christian Andersen

nce upon a time, a long, long time ago, there lived a lonely prince who set out to find a REAL princess. He looked everywhere.

He found short and tall princesses and fat and skinny princesses. He found princesses with freckles and curly hair and princesses with rosy cheeks and braids. But none was just right.

So the Prince returned to his castle, sad and alone. One night there was a most dreadful storm. Lightning lit the sky, and thunder shook the very walls of the castle!

Suddenly there came a tapping on the castle door. The Prince's mother, the Queen, opened the door to find a young maiden standing in the doorway.

The beautiful young woman said she was a REAL princess. But she didn't look like a REAL princess. Her clothes were soaked with water, which ran off her in streams and flowed out the toes of her shoes.

21

But the Prince thought she was wonderful! The Queen saw how he felt, but she wanted to be sure the maiden was truly a REAL princess. So she thought up a very special test.

Without saying a word to anyone, the Queen prepared the guest room. She piled twenty mattresses on the bed. Then she piled twenty quilts on top of the twenty mattresses. And then she took one small pea and put it *under* all the mattresses and all the quilts.

The young maiden said, "Good night," and climbed into her bed.

"How did you sleep?" asked the Queen the next morning.

"Not a wink," replied the maiden. "There was a huge rock in my bed, and I am black and blue all over."

The Queen knew immediately that she was a REAL princess. Only a REAL princess could have felt a single pea through twenty mattresses and twenty quilts!

So the Prince married the REAL Princess. Everyone in the Kingdom was invited to the wedding, and to see the famous pea that brought the Prince and Princess together at last.

MY PIGEON HOUSE

Wouldn't it be wonderful to have a house full of pretty white pigeons?
They would coo softly at night while you fell asleep.
You can play this bedtime game and pretend you have
some pigeons of your very own.

My pigeon house I open wide
And set all my pigeons free.
They fly so high they reach the sky
And alight on the tallest tree.
And when they return from their merry, merry flight,
I shut the door and say good night.
Coo-oo coo-oo coo-oo coo-oo coo-oo coo-oo
Coo coo.

My pigeon house
I open wide...

They fly so high
they reach the sky...

arms open wide

arms up

24

And alight on the
tallest tree

And when they return . . .
I shut the door

arms up, fingers down

flap hands toward yourself

And say good night.

*hands together at side of face
as if sleeping*

Little Donkey
Close Your Eyes

Little Donkey on the hill,
Standing there so very still,
Making faces at the skies—
Little Donkey, close your eyes.

Little Monkey in the tree,
Swinging there so merrily,
Throwing coconuts at the skies—
Little Monkey, close your eyes.

Silly Sheep that slowly crop,
Night has come and you must stop,
Chewing grass beneath the skies—
Silly Sheep, now close your eyes.

Little Pig that squeals about,
Make no noises with your snout,
No more squealing to the skies—
Little Pig, now close your eyes.

Wild Young Birds that sweetly sing,
Curve your heads beneath your wing,
Dark night covers all the skies—
Wild Young Birds, now close your eyes.

Old Black Cat down in the barn,
Keeping five small kittens warm,
Let the wind blow in the skies—
Dear Old Black Cat, close your eyes.

Little Child all tucked in bed,
Looking such a sleepy head,
Stars are quiet in the skies—
Little Child, now close your eyes.

Margaret Wise Brown

WEE WILLIE WINKIE

Wee Willie Winkie runs through the town,
Upstairs and downstairs in his nightgown,
Rapping at the window, crying through the lock,
"Are all the children in their beds,
for now it's eight o'clock?"

Traditional

28

Are you in bed by eight o'clock? Do you run upstairs and downstairs in your pajamas like Wee Willie? What time do you go to bed? What time would you like to go to bed? Point to the clock that shows your bedtime.

29

In the Dark

Stars

I'm glad the stars are over me
And not beneath my feet,
Where we should trample on them
Like cobbles on the street.
I think it is a happy thing
That they are set so far;
It's best to have to look up high
When you would see a star.

Traditional

31

THE SKY AT NIGHT

When you look up at the sky at night,
what is it that you see?

The Moon

The moon looks different every night.
On some nights you can see the whole
round moon. This is what we call a full
moon. On other nights, you see only half a
moon. Look up on still other nights and the
moon is just a skinny sliver.

The moon seems to shine at night.
But the moon does not really give off light.
It gets its light from the sun.
The sunlight reflects off the moon.
That's what gives the moon its glow.

The Stars

On a clear night,
you can see many stars
in the sky.

They look like little specks of light.

But the stars are even bigger
than the earth!

They look so tiny because they are very far away.

Star Pictures

Some stars seem to make pictures in the sky.
These stars make the shape of a cup with a handle.
This star picture is called the Big Dipper.
Now look straight up from the Big Dipper.
You can see a very bright star.
This is the North Star.
If you follow the North Star you will always be headed north.
People have found their way by the stars for many, many years.
Even birds watch the stars when they go south for the winter.

Look outside your window at night.
The stars are shining and making star pictures just for you!

Twinkle, Twinkle, Little Star

Twinkle, twinkle, little star,
How I wonder what you are!
Up above the world so high
Like a diamond in the sky.
Twinkle, twinkle, little star,
How I wonder what you are!

Jane Taylor

Star Light, Star Bright

Do you see a star outside your window? Make a wish on it!

Star light, star bright,
First star I see tonight,
I wish I may, I wish I might
Have the wish I wish tonight.

Traditional

Why There Is Both Day and Night

A tale told by the Ojibwa Indians

Long, long ago, when the earth was brand new, there was no difference between night and day. This was so long ago that there were no people, only birds and animals. And there was no day—only night.

Rabbit walked through the forest. It was so dark that he couldn't see where he was going. He tripped and fell over a log.

"Ouch!" cried Rabbit. "I'm tired of bumping into things. There is not enough light in the world!"

"That's not true," said a voice. "There is plenty of light."

Rabbit squinted through the darkness to see who had spoken. "Who's there?" he asked.

"Owl," said the voice. "And I say there's plenty of light in the world."

"You're wrong, Owl," said Rabbit. "I can't see a thing! It's too dark to find food! Many other animals agree with me. I will call all the animals to a council, and we'll decide whether or not there is enough light."

"Okay, Rabbit," said Owl. "I'll invite all the birds to the council, too. We'll decide this once and for all."

So Rabbit invited all the animals to the council, and Owl invited all the birds. When the time came, Rabbit brought wood for the council fire. Owl brought fire for the wood. All the birds and animals came and sat around the fire.

Rabbit began the council. "I'm sick and tired of stumbling around in the dark. We need more light in the world!" he said.

"You are right, Rabbit," said Buffalo. "We need light to help us find food. I can't see well in the dark!"

"We do not need more light," said Owl. "Too much light is dangerous."

"You are right, Owl," said Raccoon. "We need the darkness to hide from our enemies. When it is dark, we can hunt for food without becoming someone else's dinner!"

Some of the animals and birds agreed with Rabbit. Some of them agreed with Owl. Soon they were squawking and growling at each other very angrily.

"Enough!" said Rabbit, and the birds and animals grew quiet. "I'll settle this. I will use my magic to bring light into the world." Then he began to cast a spell. "Light," he said. "Light, light, light!"

"My magic is stronger than yours," said Owl. Then he began chanting, as fast as he could, "Night, night, night!"

"Light, light, light!" said Rabbit.

"Night, night, night!" said Owl.

"Watch out, Rabbit," said Buffalo. "Do not say Owl's word, or we will lose. We will have night all the time."

"Watch out, Owl," said Raccoon. "Don't say Rabbit's word! If you do, we will lose, and have light all the time."

"Light, light, light!" said Rabbit.

"Night, night, night!" said Owl.

"Go, go, go!" said all the animals and birds.

"Night," said Owl, but then his tongue slipped. "Light," he said, by accident.

"Light," said Rabbit, but at the very same time, *his* tongue slipped, and he said, "Night," quite by accident.

"We won!" cried Raccoon, for in all of the noise, he had only heard Rabbit's mistake. But then the sky lightened, and soon the world was bright. It was the dawning of the very first day on earth.

"We won!" cried Buffalo when he saw all the light.

"No," said Rabbit. "We all won, and we all lost. From now on we will have equal parts of light and dark."

And that is why we have both night and day.

Sounds at Night

My bed is warm and cozy.
Mom's tucked me in just right.
Before I go to sleep I like
to listen to the night.

Inside I hear
the steam heat hissing,
Mommy and I laughing, kissing,

clock tick-tocking,
Grandma rocking,

Grandpa snoring,
bathwater pouring,

radio static,
creakings in the attic,

telephone ringing,
pet canary singing,

faucet dripping,
cocoa-drinkers sipping.

41

Outside I hear
the car horns beeping,
sleepy birdies cheeping,

people knocking,
door unlocking,

neighbors talking,
dog-walkers walking,

window shutters flapping,
tree branches tapping...

YAWN!

My bed is warm and cozy.
My mom's turned off the light.
I think I'll close my eyes...
and ears...
and go to sleep. Good night!

Joan Israel

43

ANIMALS OF THE NIGHT

Do you ever lie in bed at night and listen to all the sounds outside? What's happening out there? You and your dog and your cat sleep at night, but some animals never sleep at night. They sleep all day, then wake up at night and go out in the dark.

Fireflies are night creatures, and they talk to each other in a special nighttime way. A male firefly lights up to call a female firefly. She lights up to answer him. They flash their lights back and forth until they find each other at last!

Owls hunt for food at night. An owl's eyes are extra big—so big that they take up most of his head! He uses his eyes to see when the moon is bright, but he finds his prey by listening, not by seeing. Owls have very good hearing.

44

Moths wait until it's dark to come out, but then they head straight for the nearest light! No one is sure why moths like to hover around lights. Maybe they think it is the sun!

Crickets come out on hot summer nights. The hotter the temperature, the faster they chirp! When the air gets cooler, crickets chirp more slowly. They are like living thermometers!

If a frog senses danger coming, he croaks out an alarm. Then all the frogs— and other animals, too— jump into the pond to hide.

Some people call raccoons "The Masked Bandits." That's because they have a mask of black fur around their eyes, and they love to steal things. They come out at night and knock over garbage cans, looking for food. They cannot see well at all. How do they find the garbage? They sniff, sniff, sniff, until it's right under their noses!

In the Dark

I've had my supper,
  And *had* my supper,
    And HAD my supper and all;
I've heard the story
  Of Cinderella,
    And how she went to the ball;
I've cleaned my teeth,
  and I've said my prayers,
    And I've cleaned and said them right;
And they've all of them been
  And kissed me lots,
    They've all of them said "Good-night."

So—here I am in the dark alone,
  There's nobody here to see;
    I think to myself,
    I play to myself,
    And nobody knows what I say to myself;
Here I am in the dark alone,
  What is it going to be?

I can think whatever I like to think,
I can play whatever I like to play,
I can laugh whatever I like to laugh,
   There's nobody here but me.

I'm talking to a rabbit . . .
   I'm talking to the sun . . .
      I think I am a hundred—
        I'm one.

I'm lying in a forest . . .
   I'm lying in a cave . . .
I'm talking to a Dragon . . .
   I'm BRAVE.
I'm lying on my left side . . .
   I'm lying on my right . . .
I'll play a lot tomorrow . . .
. . . .
I'll think a lot tomorrow . . .
. . . .
I'll laugh . . .
        a lot . . .
           tomorrow . . .
        (*Heigh-ho!*)
        Good-night

A.A. Milne

Dream Time

How They Sleep

Some things go to sleep in a funny way:
Little birds stand on one leg and tuck their heads away.
Chickens do the same, standing on their perch;
Little mice lie soft and still as if they were in church.
Kittens curl up close, in such a funny ball;
Horses hang their sleepy heads and stand still in a stall.

Sometimes dogs stretch out or curl up in a heap;
Cows lie down upon their sides when they go to sleep.
But little babies dear are snugly tucked in beds,
Warm with blankets, all so soft, and pillows for their heads.

Bird and beast and babe—I wonder which of all
Dream the dearest dreams that down from dreamland fall!

Traditional

49

Sweet Dreams, Mikey!

by Noelle Anderson

Mikey's mother tucked him in his bed.
"Sweet dreams!" she said.
"How can I get sweet dreams?" asked Mikey.
"Just close your eyes," said his mother. "A sweet dream will come to you."

"Are you sure?"

"I'm sure." Mikey's mother kissed him on the cheek and tiptoed out of his room.

Mikey lay in his big, cold bed and thought about dreams. He didn't want a dream to come to him. He wanted to pick what he dreamed about. On his window sill, he could see his stuffed brontosaurus.

"I know!" said Mikey. He climbed out of bed, got his brontosaurus, and climbed back under the covers.

"I'll dream dinosaur dreams!" Mikey stuffed the brontosaurus way under the covers to warm his feet. He closed his eyes. He imagined wading through a swamp. His feet felt cold and icky . . . that wasn't a sweet dream.

50

Mikey opened his eyes. "I know!" he said. He climbed out of bed, got his stuffed giraffe, and climbed back under the covers. "I'll dream jungle dreams!"

Mikey stuffed his giraffe under the covers. He closed his eyes. He began to imagine his neck getting longer and longer. He imagined his head getting further and further away from his body . . . that wasn't a sweet dream.

Mikey opened his eyes. "I know!" he said. He climbed out of bed, got his soccer ball, and climbed back under the covers. "I'll dream soccer dreams!"

Mikey stuffed the soccer ball under the covers. He closed his eyes. He began to imagine kicking the ball. He kicked it so hard, the ball sailed up in the air and far away . . .
that wasn't a sweet dream.

Mikey opened his eyes. "I know!" he said. He climbed out of bed, got his old rag doll, the one he'd had ever since he was born, and climbed back under the covers. "I'll dream baby dreams!"

Mikey stuffed the old rag doll under the covers. He closed his eyes. He began to imagine being seated in a high chair and eating mashed peas and carrots. Yuck! That *certainly* wasn't a sweet dream.

Mikey opened his eyes. "I know!" he said. He climbed out of bed, got his big gray cat that was sleeping near the radiator, and climbed back under the covers.

"I'll dream about you, Sneakers!"

But Sneakers didn't want to get under the covers. Mikey petted him to settle him down, and Sneakers finally went to sleep on Mikey's pillow. Then Mikey inched himself under the covers. There wasn't much room in this lumpy, bumpy bed, but at last he closed his eyes and fell asleep.

He almost didn't hear the door to his room open.

He barely heard his mother tiptoe in to check on him.

He hardly heard her click on his night-light.

But he *did* hear his mother shriek: "THERE'S A BIG, LUMPY, HAIRY-HEADED MONSTER IN MY MIKEY'S BED!"

Mikey popped his head out of the covers and said, "It's not a monster! It's me, Mikey!"

Just then, his mother opened the door to his room and peeked inside. "Are you all right, Mikey?" she asked. "I thought I heard you yelling in here."

Mikey frowned. "But weren't you just in here?" he asked.

Mikey's mother shook her head. "You must have been dreaming," she said.

Mikey threw back his covers. He climbed out of bed and put back his rag doll, his soccer ball, his giraffe, and his brontosaurus. Sneakers the cat jumped off his bed and ran out of the room.

Then Mikey climbed back under the covers. He closed his eyes.

"Sweet dreams, Mikey," said his mother.

Mikey was too tired to think about dreams. He fell asleep and dreamed about licking a triple-dipper ice cream cone . . . a sweet dream if ever there was one!

53

NIGHT WORKERS

Some people work at night while you and I are sleeping. They work in the dark of night so that our days will be safe, clean, and bright.

In the fire station, the firefighters are on duty all night long. They wait for fire alarms.

In the hospital, the night nurse gives the babies their bottles. They get hungry at night, too.

Down the street from the fire station, the baker is frosting the donuts for breakfast.

Throughout the city, police officers are on night watch. Some patrol in cars and others walk the city streets.

The tugboat captain steers a freighter safely out of the harbor.

All-night radio stations broadcast news, weather, and music to night listeners.

Pilots guide their planes in and out of the airport every night.

Milk for tomorrow's table is ready the night before. The milk-truck driver delivers the milk to stores, schools, and restaurants.

Many of our city streets are cleaned at night. The sanitation worker cleans the streets with the help of sweepers.

Wynken, Blynken and Nod

Wynken, Blynken and Nod, one night
Sailed off in a wooden shoe,
Sailed on a river of crystal light,
Into a sea of dew.
"Where are you going and what do you wish?"
The old moon asked the three.
"We have come to fish for the herring-fish
That live in the beautiful sea;
Nets of silver and gold have we,"
Said Wynken, Blynken, and Nod.

The old moon laughed and sang a song,
As they rocked in the wooden shoe,
And the wind that sped them all night long
Ruffled the waves of the dew.
The little stars were the herring-fish
That lived in the beautiful sea.
"Now cast your nets wherever you wish,
But never afeared are we"—
So cried the stars to the fishermen three:
Wynken, Blynken, and Nod.

All night long their nets they threw
To the stars in the twinkling foam,
Then down from the skies came the wooden shoe,
Bringing the fishermen home.
'Twas all so pretty a sail, it seemed
As if it could not be,
And some folks thought 'twas a dream they'd dreamed
Of sailing that beautiful sea—
But I shall name you the fishermen three:
Wynken, Blynken, and Nod.

Wynken and Blynken are two little eyes,
And Nod is a little head,
And the wooden shoe that sails the skies
Is a wee one's trundle bed.
So shut your eyes while mother sings
Of wonderful sights that be,
And you shall see the beautiful things
As you rock in the misty sea,
Where the old shoe rocked the fishermen three:
Wynken, Blynken, and Nod.

Eugene Field

59

DID YOU EVER WONDER
ABOUT DREAMS

Do dreams come true?
Dreams are not real. Even if you dream that you can fly, you won't be able to fly when you wake up! But sometimes dreams are wishes. They show us something we *want* to happen. And sometimes, if we're lucky, we get our wish. But the dream does not make it happen.

Do animals dream?
We think that animals do dream. But animals can't talk, so they can't tell us about their dreams. Sleeping dogs sometimes make funny faces and noises. Sometimes they move their legs as if they are running. Maybe they are dreaming when they do that. What do you think your pet dreams about?

Do people really walk and talk in their sleep?
It is true that many people talk in their sleep. They usually don't remember doing it, and they don't usually make much sense. And some people even get out of bed and walk in their sleep. But sleepwalking is very rare. You probably will do all your sleeping right in your very own comfy bed!

Why do we have dreams some nights and not others?
Here's a surprise. You have dreams every night. Sometimes when you wake up in the morning you can't remember dreaming at all, but you probably had at least one dream. What did you dream about last night?

Why do we have bad dreams?
Dreams are made up of things from real life. When you sleep, your mind mixes all these real-life things together to make a dream. If you're worried or scared or angry about something, you might have a bad dream. If you wake up during a bad dream, the dream seems very real. But remember, dreams are not real.

SHHH! THE MICE ARE SLEEPING

It's nighttime. The moon is bright, and everybody is asleep.
Eight little mice are sleeping, too, snug in their hiding places.
Can you find them?

Little People™ Big Book About BEDTIME

TIME-LIFE for CHILDREN™

Publisher: Robert H. Smith
Editorial Director: Neil Kagan
Associate Editor: Jean Burke Crawford
Marketing Director: Ruth P. Stevens
Promotion Director: Kathleen B. Tresnak
Associate Promotion Director: Jane B. Welihozkiy
Production Manager: Prudence G. Harris
Editorial Consultants: Jacqueline A. Ball,
          Sara Mark

PRODUCED BY PARACHUTE PRESS, INC.

Editorial Director: Joan Waricha
Editors: Christopher Medina, Jane Stine
Writers: Noelle Anderson, Joan Israel,
       Joan Powers, Jean Waricha
Designer: Deborah Michel
Illustrators: Shirley Beckes, John Speirs,
       Pat and Robin DeWitt

Time-Life Books Inc. is a wholly owned subsidiary of
Time Incorporated.

TIME-LIFE is a trademark of Time Incorporated
U.S.A.

FISHER-PRICE, LITTLE PEOPLE and AWNING
DESIGN are trademarks of Fisher-Price, Division of
The Quaker Oats Company, and are used under
license.

Time-Life Books Inc. offers a wide range of fine
publications, including home video products. For
subscription information, call 1-800-621-7026 or
write TIME-LIFE BOOKS, P.O. Box C-32068,
Richmond, Virginia 23261-2068.

ACKNOWLEDGMENTS

Every effort has been made to trace the ownership of all copyrighted material and to secure the necessary
permissions to reprint these selections. If any question arises as to the use of any material, the editor
and the publisher, while expressing regret for any inadvertent error, will make the necessary correction
in future printings.

Grateful acknowledgment is made to the following for permission to reprint copyrighted material: EP Dutton,
a division of Penguin Books USA, Inc. for "In the Dark" from NOW WE ARE SIX by A.A. Milne, copyright
© 1927 by EP Dutton, renewed 1955 by A.A. Milne. Harper & Row for "Little Donkey Close Your Eyes" from
NIBBLE, NIBBLE by Margaret Wise Brown, copyright © 1959 by William R. Scott, Inc., copyright renewed
1987 by Roberta Brown Rauch. McClelland & Stewart Ltd. for Canadian rights to "In the Dark" from NOW
WE ARE SIX by A.A. Milne, copyright © 1955 by A.A. Milne. Methuen Children's Books for United Kingdom
rights to "In the Dark" from NOW WE ARE SIX by A.A. Milne, copyright © 1955 by A.A. Milne. Mary Chute
Smith for "Going to Bed" from RHYMES ABOUT US by Marchette Chute, copyright © 1974 by EP Dutton.

Library of Congress Cataloging-in-Publication Data

Little people big book about bedtime.
    p. cm.—(Little people big books)
    Summary: A collection of original stories, folktales, essays, questions and answers, poems, activities, and
games relating to bedtime.
    ISBN 0-8094-7454-9.—ISBN 0-8094-7455-7 (lib. bdg.)
    1. Bedtime—Literary collections. [1. Bedtime—Literary collections.] I. Time-Life for Children (Firm)
  II. Title: About bedtime. III. Series.
PZ5.L7256 1989
808.8'033—dc20.

89-5093
CIP
AC

TIME-LIFE BOOKS
ALEXANDRIA, VIRGINIA

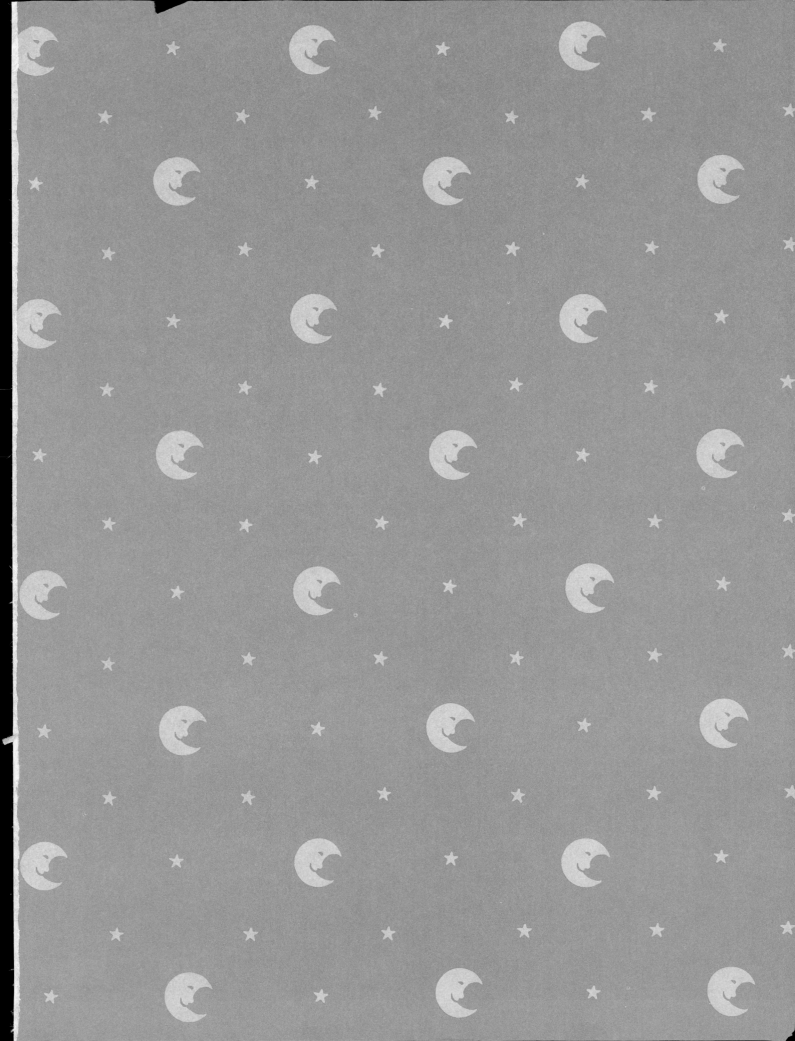

Bedtime

All day in Mother's garden here
I play and play and play.
But when night brings a dozen stars
I can no longer stay.

Sometimes the sun has hardly set
Before the stars begin.
A dozen stars come out so fast
And then I must go in.

I count them very carefully,
Especially 'round the moon,
Because I do not wish to go
To bed a star too soon.

Helen Coale Crew